BIGGEST NAMES IN SPORTS
AARON JUDGE
BASEBALL STAR

by Greg Bates

WWW.FOCUSREADERS.COM

Focus Readers is distributed by North Star Editions:
sales@northstareditions.com | 888-417-0195

Produced for Focus Readers by Red Line Editorial.

Photographs ©: Frank Franklin II/AP Images, cover, 1, 22–23, 25; Kyodo/AP Images, 4–5; Lynne Sladky/AP Images, 7, 9; Seth Poppel/Yearbook Library, 10–11, 13; Brian Westerholt/Four Seam Images/AP Images, 15; Bill Kostroun/AP Images, 16–17, 18; Julie Jacobson/AP Images, 21; Kathy Willens/AP Images, 26; Red Line Editorial, 29

ISBN
978-1-63517-867-8 (hardcover)
978-1-63517-968-2 (paperback)
978-1-64185-171-8 (ebook pdf)
978-1-64185-070-4 (hosted ebook)

Library of Congress Control Number: 2018931679

Printed in the United States of America
Mankato, MN
May, 2018

ABOUT THE AUTHOR

Greg Bates is a freelance sports journalist based in Green Bay, Wisconsin. He has covered the Green Bay Packers for nearly a decade. He has also written for outlets such as *USA Today Sports Weekly*, the Associated Press, and USA Hockey.

TABLE OF CONTENTS

CHAPTER 1

Home Run Hero 5

CHAPTER 2

Three-Sport Star 11

CHAPTER 3

Immediate Impact 17

CHAPTER 4

Postseason Performer 23

At-a-Glance Map • 28
Focus on Aaron Judge • 30
Glossary • 31
To Learn More • 32
Index • 32

HOME RUN HERO

With a huge swing, Aaron Judge launched the ball into the stands. The New York Yankees slugger was making a major splash at the 2017 Home Run Derby. The derby is a contest held during the **All-Star break**. Eight of the game's biggest hitters were taking part.

Judge takes a mighty swing at the Home Run Derby.

Each player had four minutes to hit as many home runs as possible.

In the derby's first round, Judge was up against Miami Marlins star Justin Bour. And Bour had swatted an impressive 22 home runs. That put the pressure on Judge to hit more. Judge

WHAT'S BEHIND A NUMBER?

Most major league players wear numbers between 1 and 50. Young players are usually given high numbers during **spring training**. That's because there are a lot of players on the roster at that time. During the spring of 2016, Judge was given No. 99. He decided to keep that number when he was called up to the majors.

Judge watches the ball fly after crushing one of his many home runs at the 2017 derby.

didn't disappoint. With each swing, his confidence grew. He finished the first round with 23 homers.

In the next round, Judge took on fellow **rookie** Cody Bellinger. The Los Angeles Dodgers star cranked out 12 home runs.

Now it was Judge's turn. He hit his 13th homer with more than a minute left on the clock. He was headed to the derby's final round.

Now Judge faced off against Minnesota Twins slugger Miguel Sanó. With only 10 home runs, Sanó had a disappointing round. Judge needed only 11 home runs to become the 2017 champ. He had four minutes to show what he could do. His first three swings were all homers. Then, near the two-minute mark, Judge hit his 11th home run to claim the title.

Standing 6 feet 7 inches (201 cm) tall and weighing 282 pounds (128 kg), Judge is one of the biggest players in Major

Judge's teammates soak him in water to celebrate his derby victory.

League Baseball (MLB). The Yankees star is used to crushing the ball. And that's exactly what he did at the 2017 Home Run Derby.

CHAPTER 2

THREE-SPORT STAR

Aaron Judge was born on April 26, 1992, in Linden, California. He was adopted as a baby. In high school, Aaron was a three-sport star. He excelled at football, basketball, and baseball.

On the baseball field, Aaron played first base and pitcher. He was one of the top pitchers in the state of California.

A young Aaron Judge takes a shot during a high school basketball game.

He was also great at bat, even back then. But most teams walked Aaron when he came up to the plate. They were afraid he would hit a home run.

Many MLB **scouts** were becoming interested in Aaron's skills. The Oakland Athletics drafted him after his senior

RECRUITED TO PLAY FOOTBALL

Aaron was a beast on the football field. As a senior in high school, he scored 17 touchdowns. College football programs took notice. Aaron received several **scholarship** offers. The schools included football powers such as Notre Dame and Stanford. But Aaron wasn't interested in playing college football. He was focused on baseball.

Aaron Judge (2) towered above his teammates on the football field.

year of high school. But Aaron knew he was not ready to play in the majors. He believed he would improve more by playing at the college level. He accepted a scholarship from Fresno State.

During his sophomore year at Fresno State, Judge helped lead his team to the College World Series. He also won the College Home Run Derby. Once again, Judge was on the pro scouts' radar.

After Judge's junior year in 2013, the New York Yankees selected him in the MLB draft. Rather than finishing college, he decided to join the Yankees. Judge still wasn't ready for the major leagues, though. He spent three seasons playing for the Yankees' minor league teams.

Judge started in the minors with the Tampa Yankees. He also played for the Charleston RiverDogs and the Trenton Thunder. During this time, he worked

Judge runs the bases during a minor league game with the Charleston RiverDogs.

on being a better hitter and all-around player. His dream of playing in the majors was within sight.

CHAPTER 3

IMMEDIATE IMPACT

Late in the 2016 season, the Yankees called Judge up to the major leagues. His first game was at Yankee Stadium in New York. Judge stepped up to the plate in his first at bat. The pitcher threw two quick strikes. But on the third pitch, Judge liked what he saw. He swung hard.

Judge swings for the fences in his first major league at bat.

Judge's teammates congratulate him after his first major league home run.

The ball sailed high and deep over the center field wall. It was a home run!

The ball landed in Monument Park. That's where the Yankees have **plaques** honoring their greatest players of all time. Judge was only the fifth Yankee to homer in his first plate appearance. He hit three more home runs that year. Yankees fans were excited to see what the next season would bring.

Judge worked hard in the off-season. He went into spring training trying to impress the coaches. And he did just that. Judge was **consistent** at the plate and made good contact with the ball. In the minors, Judge had struck out a lot. But now, he put the ball in play. Judge made the Yankees' opening day roster in 2017. He would be the team's starting right fielder.

Judge made every game count. In the first half of the season, he smacked 30 home runs. That led all MLB players. During the midpoint of the season, he also won the Home Run Derby.

Pitchers had to be careful how they threw to Judge. Because of his ability to hit long balls, pitchers didn't give him many good pitches. Even so, Judge hit 22 homers in the second half of the season. That gave him a total of 52 for the year. Only the Marlins' Giancarlo Stanton hit more home runs that year, with a total of 59. Judge set an MLB record for rookies. He broke the record of 49 that Mark McGwire set in 1987.

Judge (right) celebrates with a teammate after making an out.

Judge's spectacular year helped the Yankees reach the **postseason**. Now Yankees fans were counting on Judge to help the team when it mattered most.

CHAPTER 4

POSTSEASON PERFORMER

Aaron Judge was playing in the first postseason game of his career. The Yankees faced the Minnesota Twins in the 2017 American League (AL) Wild Card Game. The winner would advance to the AL Division Series. For the losing team, the season would be over.

Judge proved to be a valuable hitter in the 2017 Wild Card Game.

Judge made his way to the batter's box. It was the fourth inning, and he wanted to extend his team's 5–4 lead. On the first pitch, he took a strike. But on the next pitch, Judge connected with a curveball. It was a line drive that sailed over the left fielder's head. The ball cleared the fence and landed in the first row of the stands.

Judge's home run helped the Yankees win the game 8–4. He had shown how valuable he was to his team. It was the Yankees' first postseason win in five years.

In the AL Division Series, the Yankees squared off against the Cleveland Indians. Judge struggled in the series,

Judge rounds the bases after clobbering a home run.

with just one hit in five games. But the Yankees came out on top. They defeated the Indians three games to two.

Now the Yankees faced the Houston Astros in the AL Championship Series.

Judge swats a home run against the Houston Astros.

Judge swatted three home runs in the series, but they weren't enough. Houston won the series in seven games.

It was a disappointing end to the season. But no one could deny that

Judge's career had started out with a bang. He was the **unanimous** winner of the AL Rookie of the Year Award. The future looked bright for the young Yankees slugger.

RARE COMPANY FOR A ROOKIE

Judge joined great company when he was named AL Rookie of the Year. He became the ninth Yankees player to do it. Legendary shortstop Derek Jeter was the last Yankee to win the award. Judge also came close to winning the AL Most Valuable Player (MVP) Award. Only two players in history have won both awards in the same season. Fred Lynn did it in 1975, and Ichiro Suzuki accomplished the feat in 2001.

AARON JUDGE

- Height: 6 feet 7 inches (201 cm)
- Weight: 282 pounds (128 kg)
- Birth date: April 26, 1992
- Birthplace: Linden, California
- High school: Linden High School (Linden, California)
- College: Fresno State (2011–2013)
- Minor league teams: Tampa Yankees (2014); Charleston RiverDogs (2014); Trenton Thunder (2015)
- MLB team: New York Yankees (2016–)
- Major awards: 2017 Home Run Derby champion; 2017 American League Rookie of the Year

Linden

New York

Trenton

Fresno

Charleston

Tampa

FOCUS ON
AARON JUDGE

Write your answers on a separate piece of paper.

1. Write a sentence that summarizes Judge's performance in the 2017 postseason.

2. Do you think Aaron should have taken a football scholarship? Why or why not?

3. Which team did the Yankees beat in the 2017 Wild Card Game?

    A. Minnesota Twins
    B. Houston Astros
    C. Oakland Athletics

4. In the final round of the Home Run Derby, why did Judge stop swinging near the two-minute mark?

    A. He was too tired to keep going.
    B. He had already won the derby.
    C. He didn't think he could win.

Answer key on page 32.

GLOSSARY

All-Star break
A time during the middle of the season when the best players compete in various activities, including the All-Star Game.

consistent
Happening in the same way time after time.

plaques
Signs that describe important people or events.

postseason
A set of games played after the regular season to decide which team will be the champion.

rookie
A professional athlete in his or her first year.

scholarship
Money given to a student to pay for education expenses.

scouts
People whose jobs involve looking for talented young players.

spring training
A time when players get ready for the upcoming season.

unanimous
Having agreement from all voters.

TO LEARN MORE

BOOKS

Howell, Brian. *New York Yankees*. Minneapolis: Abdo
  Publishing, 2015.
Kelley, K. C. *New York Yankees*. New York: AV2 by Weigl,
  2018.
Williams, Doug. *12 Reasons to Love the New York Yankees*.
  Mankato, MN: 12-Story Library, 2016.

NOTE TO EDUCATORS

Visit **www.focusreaders.com** to find lesson plans,
activities, links, and other resources related to this title.

INDEX

Bellinger, Cody, 7
Bour, Justin, 6

Cleveland Indians, 24
College World Series,
  14

Fresno State, 13–14

Home Run Derby, 5–9,
  20
Houston Astros, 25–26

Linden, California, 11
Lynn, Fred, 27

McGwire, Mark, 20
Minnesota Twins, 8, 23
minor leagues, 14, 19

New York Yankees, 5, 9,
  14, 17–19, 21, 23–25,
  27
Notre Dame, 12

Oakland Athletics, 12

Rookie of the Year
  Award, 27

Sanó, Miguel, 8
Stanford, 12
Stanton, Giancarlo, 20
Suzuki, Ichiro, 27

Yankee Stadium, 17

Answer Key: 1. Answers will vary; 2. Answers will vary; 3. A; 4. B